D1537596

SUPER SANDCASTLE

Animal Habitats

What Lives in Streams and Rivers?

Oona Gaarder-Juntti

Consulting Editor, Diane Craig, M.A./Reading Specialist

ABDO
Publishing Company

Published by ABDO Publishing Company, 8000 West 78th Street, Edina, Minnesota 55439. Copyright © 2009 by Abdo Consulting Group, Inc. International copyrights reserved in all countries. No part of this book may be reproduced in any form without written permission from the publisher. Super SandCastle™ is a trademark and logo of ABDO Publishing Company.

Printed in the United States.

Credits
Editor: Liz Salzmann
Content Developer: Nancy Tuminelly
Cover and Interior Design and Production: Oona Gaarder-Juntti, Mighty Media
Illustration: Oona Gaarder-Juntti
Photo Credits: AbleStock, © Biosphoto/BIOS; Cole Brandon/Peter Arnold Inc., Digital Vision, Nicole Duplaix/Getty Images, ShutterStock

Library of Congress Cataloging-in-Publication Data

Gaarder-Juntti, Oona, 1979-

What lives in streams and rivers? / Oona Gaarder-Juntti.

p. cm. -- (Animal habitats)

ISBN 978-1-60453-171-8

1. Stream animals--Juvenile literature. 2. Stream ecology--Juvenile literature. 3. Rivers--Juvenile literature. I. Title.

QL145.G23 2009

578.76'4--dc22

2008015359

Super SandCastle™ books are created by a team of professional educators, reading specialists, and content developers around five essential components—phonemic awareness, phonics, vocabulary, text comprehension, and fluency—to assist young readers as they develop reading skills and strategies and increase their general knowledge. All books are written, reviewed, and leveled for guided reading, early reading intervention, and Accelerated Reader® programs for use in shared, guided, and independent reading and writing activities to support a balanced approach to literacy instruction.

About SUPER SANDCASTLE™

Bigger Books for Emerging Readers
Grades K–4

Created for library, classroom, and at-home use, Super SandCastle™ books support and engage young readers as they develop and build literacy skills and will increase their general knowledge about the world around them. Super SandCastle™ books are part of SandCastle™, the leading PreK–3 imprint for emerging and beginning readers. Super SandCastle™ features a larger trim size for more reading fun.

Let Us Know
Super SandCastle™ would like to hear your stories about reading this book. What was your favorite page? Was there something hard that you needed help with? Share the ups and downs of learning to read. We want to hear from you! Send us an e-mail.

sandcastle@abdopublishing.com

Contact us for a complete list of SandCastle™, Super SandCastle™, and other nonfiction and fiction titles from ABDO Publishing Company.

www.abdopublishing.com • 8000 West 78th Street Edina, MN 55439 • 800-800-1312 • 952-831-1632 fax

Streams and rivers are bodies of water that flow in one direction. Many rivers start in the mountains where water from melting snow flows downhill. Other rivers flow out of springs or lakes.

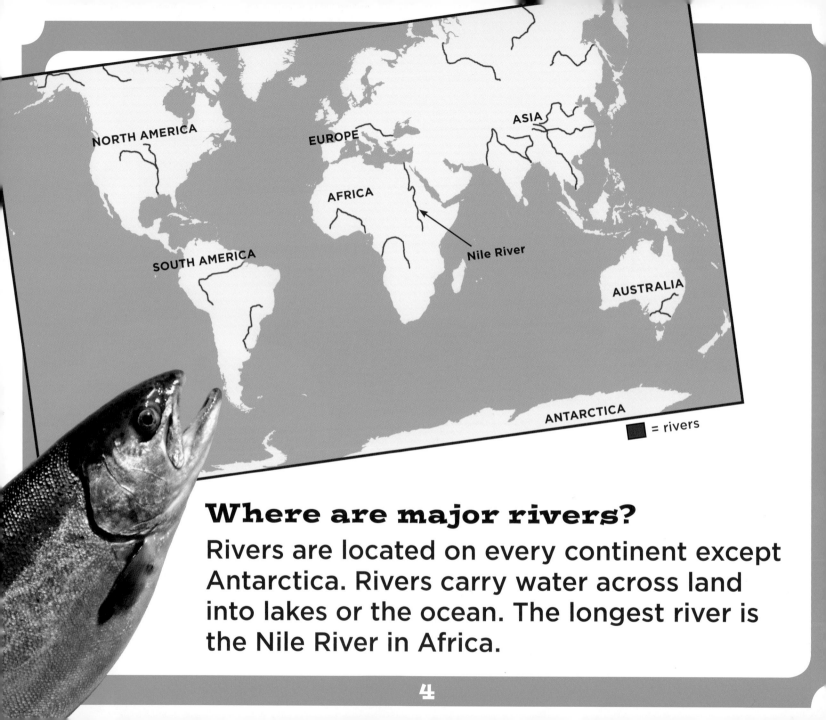

NORTH AMERICA

EUROPE

ASIA

AFRICA

SOUTH AMERICA

Nile River

AUSTRALIA

ANTARCTICA

■ = rivers

Where are major rivers?

Rivers are located on every continent except Antarctica. Rivers carry water across land into lakes or the ocean. The longest river is the Nile River in Africa.

What do streams and rivers look like?

The water in a stream or river flows in a narrow channel. The sides of the channel are called banks. Many different plants and animals live in or near streams and rivers.

AMERICAN BULLFROG

Animal class: Reptile
Location: North America

The American bullfrog is the largest frog in North America. They can be up to eight inches long and weigh more than one pound. Males have a loud, deep call that sounds like a bull.

Bullfrogs sit and wait for prey to pass by. They eat insects, mice, fish, birds, snakes, and other frogs.

WOOD DUCK

Animal class: Bird
Location: North America

Wood ducks make their nests in trees near water. The ducklings safely jump from as high as 290 feet out of their nests. Wood ducks eat insects, seeds, fruits, and water plants.

Male wood ducks are brightly colored. Females have gray and brown feathers.

SOCKEYE SALMON

Animal class: Fish
Location: Northern Pacific Ocean

Sockeye salmon are born in rivers. They move to the ocean after about three years. Adults return to the river to lay their eggs. Some salmon swim more than 1,000 miles upstream.

The sockeye salmon's body turns bright red when it is breeding.

BEAVER

Animal class: Mammal
Location: North America, Europe, and Asia

Beavers have sharp teeth that they use to cut down trees. They build homes called lodges out of sticks and mud. The entrance is underwater to keep other animals out.

Beavers also build dams across streams and rivers. The dams can change the rivers into lakes or wetlands.

River Otter

Animal class: Mammal
Location: North America, South America, Europe, Asia, and Africa

River otters have soft, thick fur that keeps them warm in the water. They are good at swimming and diving. They can hold their breath up to eight minutes underwater.

River otters catch their prey with their teeth. They bring their catch to the riverbank to eat.

GREAT BLUE HERON

Animal class: Bird
Location: North America

Great blue herons are the largest herons in North America. They have long necks and legs. They wade along the banks of streams looking for snakes, frogs, fish, or mice to eat.

Great blue herons can be more than four feet tall. Their wingspan can be more than six feet.

PLATYPUS

Animal class: **Mammal**
Location: **Australia**

Platypuses have four webbed feet, a rubbery bill, and a flat tail. Platypuses are mammals even though they lay eggs. Female platypuses dig burrows and lay one to three eggs.

Platypuses use their bills to dig for food on the bottom of the river. They eat insects, worms, and shellfish.

NILE CROCODILE

Animal class: Reptile
Location: Africa

Nile crocodiles can be up to 20 feet long. Some weigh more than 1,600 pounds! A Nile crocodile can eat half its body weight at a time. But it only needs to eat about once a week.

Nile crocodiles mostly eat fish. They sometimes prey on larger animals such as zebras, buffalo, and baboons.

Have you ever been to a stream or a river?

More Stream and River Animals

Can you learn about these stream and river animals?

bald eagle

bass

brown bear

cormorant

cottonmouth snake

egret

gladiator fish

hippopotamus

leech

mandarin duck

mink

muskrat

nutria

raccoon

rainbow trout

salamander

snail

sturgeon

GLOSSARY

breed – to create offspring, or babies.

burrow – a hole or tunnel dug in the ground by a small animal for use as shelter.

continent – one of seven large land masses on earth. The continents are Asia, Africa, Europe, North America, South America, Australia, and Antarctica.

mammal – a warm-blooded animal that has hair and whose females produce milk to feed the young.

shellfish – an aquatic animal that has a hard shell, such as a clam or lobster.

spring – a place where water comes up out of the ground.

upstream – the opposite direction from the flow of water.

webbed – having skin connecting the fingers or toes.

wetland – a low, wet area of land such as a swamp or a marsh.

wingspan – the distance from one wing tip to the other when the wings are fully spread.